T0070216

The Little Inspiration Book

Ideas to Empower Women

by DEB

First Edition

ISBN: 978-1-5536-9420-5 (sc)

Trafford rev. 05/09/2022

 www.trafford.com

North America & international
toll-free: 844-688-6899 (USA & Canada)
fax: 812 355 4082

Acknowledgements

This book is dedicated to Jenn, thank you for standing by my side all these years.

♥

Thank you to Sally for inspiring me to write this book and supporting me throughout. Thank you SARK for your book *Wild Succulent Women* which ignited the belief in myself to create my vision. Thank you to Matt for believing in me right from the start and for all your technical help.

♥

This book would not have been possible without the help, words of encouragement, ideas, suggestions, editing, and support from: Sally Horton, Catherine Broom, Paula Lepak, Chantelle Giroday, Shannon Tong, Jennifer Waterhouse, Heather Von-Hauff, Katrina Mitchell, Heidi Pass, Matt Chaney, Chris Chan, Jessica Lindy and Heidi Kussman.

DEB and Telly on a backpacking trip on Mt. Aarosmith, Vancouver Island, British Columbia, Canada.

Every wilderness trip gives me new energy and rejuvenates my spirit.

Table of Contents

Table of Contents

Part Three - Try This! (cont'd)

My Story

One night several years ago, tears streamed down my face as I sat curled up in the empty bathtub of my apartment. I was ready to give up on my life. Not knowing what else to do, I called my friend Sally.

"Deb," Sally said, "You've got so many wonderful projects, ideas, and talents - things to live for. There are some amazing people in your life. Write them down and look at this list whenever you feel this low." This is how *The Little Inspiration Book* began.

After the bathtub episode and my talk with Sally, my life changed dramatically. I wrote down a list of projects to do, dreams I wanted to live, and people who I could call for support when I needed it.

I spent the next three years taking risks, following my heart, and living my dreams. I went on wilderness backpacking trips, camping trips, and retreats by myself. I realized my dream of cycle touring in Iceland and spent an entire summer alone, having the adventure of a life time. Still hungry for more, the next year I sailed from Canada to Mexico working as crew on various sailboats for room and board.

During my travelling and adventuring I continued to write fastidiously in my journals adding more thoughts and ideas to the *Little Inspiration Book*. Through writing I learned about myself, my passions, what made me happy, and what made me feel sad or depressed. I learned the joy in expressing my truth, following my dreams, and living as an empowered and independent woman.

This book is full of the ideas, thoughts, stories, suggestions, exercises, quotes and resources that helped me on my path. I pass them onto you in the hopes that perhaps one or more ideas will motivate you, inspire you, and encourage you to make your own life extraordinary.

"I go where no road goes and the road will go with me."
- Ancient Chinese saying

Love,

DEB

Part One - Rejuvenate

Warming up for karate class

Every class teaches me something new and
challenges me in a different way.

Move Your Body

Exercise has so many benefits to your mind, body, and spirit. Keeping active heightens your sense of being alive and feeling happy. Movement pumps natural endorphins through your body, keeps your blood circulating, stimulates your heart, increases oxygen flow within your body, keeps you trim, cleans out your pores, and encourages the elimination of toxins. What better medicine could exist?

- **Get moving on your own.** Make a point of adding movement into your day; dance to some tunes at home, walk to the corner grocery store, or bike to work or school.
- **Make a date with a friend to do exercise.** Play racquet ball, go walking, roller blading or skating, weight lifting, running, canoeing, hiking, skiing, rowing, or bike riding.
- **Try a class at your local gym or community center.** Try a class in dancing, aerobics, weight lifting, kick boxing, or water aerobics.
- **Join a team or league.** Investigate group sports available in your community. You could join a team in tennis, soccer, basketball, volleyball, hockey, or water polo.
- **Practice ancient body movements.** Experiment with Yoga, Tai chi, belly dancing, or Chi Gung.
- **Participate in martial arts.** Try a class in Tae Kwon Do, Karate, Jujitsu, Akedo, or Judo.

I became passionate about karate at the age of twenty participating in my first summer training at a school in White Rock, British Columbia, Canada. For two months that summer there were over eighty adults and children participating in the training that took place five evenings each week and on Saturdays. Each class was held at a different outdoor location, the instructor using the natural surroundings to challenge and teach us. The beach was a favorite training location. If the tide was out we would do kata (sequenced forms) on the flat sandy area, run the length of the beach, and move into the water to practice basic techniques and self-defense. If the tide was up we would perch ourselves on large boulders lining the beach and precariously do kicks and punches trying not to loose our balance and fall off. Other classes were held at local parks and would consist of hopping one-legged up hundreds of wooden stairs, dizzily rolling down grassy hills to get up as quickly as possible and perform the next technique - jumping through tires laid out on a field. I'll never forget one Saturday morning class where we ran along a muddy forest trail alongside a river. To my complete dismay I was expected to roll in the mud! At every mud puddle I encountered I had to shoulder roll through it. I would brace myself, closing my eyes as the cold wet mud soaked my clothing. Then I'd emerge wet, dirty, and laughing. On our way back along the trail, the instructor decided we needed to clean off. The braver members of our group obliged and jumped off a small cliff into icy cold river waters. I loved the feeling of community I had with all the members of the school. In particular, I felt an immediate kinship with the women of our group. Because of the children that joined us, every practice felt like being part of a big family. Many times that summer I was pushed to my physical limits, yet I always felt supported and encouraged to not give up.   After that summer I joined a karate club where I was attending school and continued with my training. Seven years later I am invigorated, challenged, and motivated as I continue my practice.

♥

"Enjoy your body. Use it every way you can. Don't be afraid of it or of what other people think of it. It's the greatest instrument you'll ever own."

- Kurt Vonnegut

RESOURCES

- *Body for Life,* Bill Phillips
- The form of karate I practice is called Kyokushin Karate. This website, based in Australia, will provide you with details and has links to karate schools all over the world: http://argus.appsci.unsw.edu.au/karate.
- I have written some stories about training karate at different schools I stopped at during my trip sailing from Canada to Mexico. To access the stories please click in the 'about DEB' section at www.debcreative.com.

Schedule a Sacred Day

Plan one day a week to do something for yourself to nourish your soul. Use this time to remember your dreams and ideas. Schedule this day in your daybook.

- **Chill out.** Relax, do nothing, sit in a comfy chair. Stay in bed all day; don't get out of your pajamas, snuggle up with extra blankets, and bring a mug of tea or hot chocolate to bed. Meditate. Write in your journal. Read inspirational books or a novel. Take naps all day. No housework allowed!
- **Pamper yourself.** Soak your feet in a tub of hot water mixed with epsom salts, lavender and tea-tree oil. Go for a massage, energy healing, sauna, shiatsu, or a foot massage. Get a manicure & manicure. Take a hot bath, surround your-self with candles, and play your favorite tunes.
- **Treat yourself.** Buy yourself a gift and wrap it up. Buy yourself flowers. Prepare a special meal at home or eat out. Make or purchase your favorite snack foods and indulge.
- **Find out.** Get a tarot card or psychic reading. Pull a *Ruin* stone or an animal card. Visit a fortune teller or palm reader.
- **Explore.** Go on an adventure in your neighborhood. Walk down new streets. Go into stores you've never explored, visit a local plant nursery, or tour a museum. Plan a local bike ride, a hike, or a picnic at a local park. Take a pottery or art class. Listen to an orchestra rehearsal.
- **Get outside.** Be alone in a park or at the beach. Hike in a local forest or park. Sit or walk by a lake, a stream, or the

ocean and listen to the water. Watch birds and butterflies. Plant a garden or pot some flowers. Go for a walk and smell flowers along the way. Go out and look at the moon and the stars. Watch the sun rise or set. Listen to the rain.

- **Create.** Write a letter to a friend or yourself. Paint, draw, color, sculpt, or sketch. Make ornaments, decorations, or crafts according for the season - Christmas tree ornaments, door wreaths, painted easter eggs, handmade soaps and lotions, dried flower bouquets, gift cards, or potpourri.
- **Laugh.** Watch a comedy or magic show - live or on TV. Read a book by Ben Elton or Bill Cosby. Subscribe to the *Funny Times*. Sing out loud in the shower or tub. Dance naked around your house to your favorite upbeat music. Watch children play.

Feeling a little down and out and uninspired to work, I spent an evening last week flipping through a stack of magazines. As I paged through the vibrant glossy pages, I cut out inspirational quotes and photographs. I found a wonderful picture of my dream cabin. I selected pictures of flowers I wanted to have in my home. Within the colourful magazines, I found a beautiful photograph depicting a scene of a place I would love to hike and explore. I cut out pictures of decorative art pieces and a desk that would be perfect for my studio. I then pasted all these clippings into my journal. (See the illustration on page 72.) After cutting up six magazines I felt energized and excited about my dreams and future visions. Taking those couple of hours to play revived me. The next day I continued my work where previously I had been stuck.

**Take time to think
It is the source of all power**

**Take time to play
It is the secret of perpetual youth**

**Take time to read
It is the fountain of wisdom**

**Take time to pray
It is the greatest power on earth**

**Take time to love and be loved
It is a God-given privilege**

**Take time to be friendly
It is the road to happiness**

**Take time to laugh
It is the music of the soul**

**Take time to give
It is too short a day to be selfish**

**Take time to work
It is the price of success.**

- author unknown

RESOURCES

- *Power Thought Cards,* Louis Hay
- *The Animal Cards: The Discovery of Power Through the Ways of Animals,* Jamie Sams & David Carson
- *Oprah Magazine*

You are What You Eat

When you nourish your body with whole, natural foods, giving yourself the best nutrients available, you build a strong mind and body, whistle creating emotional balance and harmony. The importance of eating well cannot be overstated.

♥

- **Choose whole foods over processed foods.** During the manufacturing process, foods become devoid of nutrients, fiber, vitamins, and minerals. Foods that have not been altered or preserved are whole foods and contain all the nutrients we need - naturally!
- **Eat whole foods.** Include fresh vegetables and fruits regularly in your diet. Eat broccoli, asparagus, bok choy, spinach, salads, bananas, apples, pears, oranges, potatoes, yams, and whole grains such as brown rice, quinoa, buckwheat, barley, spelt, and whole wheat bread. Garnish dishes with sunflower seeds, almonds, and pumpkin seeds. Make meals with beans such as aduki, mung, chick peas, black beans, string beans, lima, and pinto beans.
- **Eliminate refined foods.** Processed foods contain adverse chemicals that are a detriment to your long term health. Foods such as potato chips, doughnuts, sugar drenched cereal, baked goods such as cookies and cakes, ice-cream, hot dogs, white bread, processed meats & cheese, fried foods, soda pop, and canned foods are all best avoided.
- **Check labels.** Look for added artificial colors, flavours, sweeteners, and preservatives. All these added chemicals

are poison to your body and do not contribute to your health and well-being.

- **Detoxify your body internally.** Various foods, teas and herbs are useful to cleanse your body. Add fiber to your diet by eating fresh fruits and vegetables, ground up flax seeds, and black sesame seeds. Dandelion tea which is known to detoxify the liver. Try Avena Originals' *Herb Cocktail* a mixture of herbs which act to cleanse and detoxify the digestive system. See page 16.
- **Drink water.** Water replenishes your body with fluid and minerals, lubricates your joints & digestive system, re-hydrates your body, and flushes out toxins. It's the *best* drink available. For a comparable alternative drink herbal teas, green tea, and water with freshly squeezed lemon added.
- **Detoxify your body externally.** Activities that induce sweating help to clean out toxins via our skin. Exercise! Sweat! Take a sauna. Add Epsom salts to a hot bath. Burn lavender and eucalyptus aromatherapy. Participate in a sweat lodge. Swim in the ocean.
- **Choose organic produce.** Eating organically grown foods eliminates the unnecessary intake of pesticides and chemicals into your body.
- **Plan ahead.** Prepare snacks ahead of time to encourage healthful eating in stressful times. Carrot and celery sticks, radishes, pickles, yogurt, fruit and nut bars, dried figs, pumpkin and sunflower seeds, bananas, raisins and apples all make great snacks.

♥

During a six week mountaineering course I learned by experience the effect food and water on my outlook and performance. This trip with Outward Bound was my first exposure to extended winter camping. There were ten of us in the group and during this course we crossed glaciers, passed through potential avalanche areas, navigated through a white out, rock climb and scaled mountains. Besides learning new skills and how to use ropes, ice axes and harnesses, simple day to day living was a challenge. Temperatures were often below freezing. We were up everyday at 4:30 am in the cold and dark pulling on frozen clothes and packing our bags. After breakfast we put our 30-40 pound packs on our backs and hiked 5 - 15 kilometers (3-9 miles) each day. Every morning the group leaders always encouraged us to drink one liter of water before heading out each day. I also made a point of eating small snacks throughout the day. When I was hydrated and well fed my energy remained more consistent and my outlook more positive than those mornings when I skipped drinking water and days when I missed snacks.

♥

**"If you wish to follow a healthy diet,
follow this simple rule:
Never eat anything made in a factory...
Read the small print on all packaged food items,
and if the substances mentioned are chemicals,
leave them alone."**
-from a natural health magazine

RESOURCES

- *Fit for Life,* Harvey and Marilyn Diamond
- *Perfect Health,* Deepak Chopra
- *8 Weeks to Optimum Health* and *Spontaneous Healing,* Andrew Weil
- *Healing with Whole Foods,* Paul Pitchford
- *Hard to Swallow - The Truth About Food Additives,* D. Sarjeant and K. Evans
- *Avena Originals* health products. Phone: 1-800-207-2239, E-mail: avena@telusplanet.net, Website: http://www.avenaoriginals.com.

Spend Time in Nature

Take some time this week and go somewhere outside that is special and sacred for you. Spending time in a beautiful place outdoors can uplift your spirit, calm your nerves, and offer tranquility from today's hectic world.

♥

Get outside...

- **Enjoy the tranquility of nature.** Star gaze, observe a waterfall, sit by the ocean or a gurgling stream. Observe plants, flowers, and rocks with a magnifying glass. Look at sea life in ocean tidal pools. Paint or draw in 'plein airs' the natural landscape.
- **With yourself.** Walk by the ocean. Sit by a lake. Watch a river. Hike up a mountain. Plan and go on a solo overnight camping trip or day hike. Walk in a local forest or park. Sit on the grass in a park or in your backyard.
- **With friends.** Go camping, hiking, or mountaineering. Join a guided expedition or trip. Go on a kayaking, river rafting, horse back riding or canoeing trip.
- **With your family.** Plan a family camping trip; involve everyone with preparations such as choosing the destination, camp activities, and meal planning.
- **Participate in an outdoors club.** Join a walking, hiking, bird watching or natural history club. Take an Outward Bound or other outdoor course.

- **Be active outdoors.** With yourself, friends, or a group go swimming, running, walking, rowing, surfing, rock climbing, kayaking, or cycling outdoors.

My parents got me hooked on spending time in the outdoors starting from when I was a little girl. Each summer we used to drive through British Columbia, Canada to various camping locations near a river. During the day my dad would white water kayak with his friends while I would play. I remember swimming in calm sections of the river while yelling out to my mom, "This is like swimming in a bottle of mineral water!" On warm days I would jump from river boulder to boulder, the aim was not to fall in or get my feet wet. Sometimes I would draw water paintings on the rocks. The evenings were filled with campfires and roasted marshmallows. Later, my parents would bundle me up with sweaters and jackets until I was double in size. Then my dad and I would get away from the lights to look for planets and star clusters with his telescope. We would stay out star gazing while simultaneously having a "stay warm" competition, waiting to see who would get cold first. I will always remember the night

I won the contest and outlasted my dad. I also developed a passion and love for being in the outdoors.

♥

"Nature has been for me, for as long as I can remember, a source of solace, inspiration, adventure, and delight, a home, a teacher, a companion."
-Lorraine Anderson

RESOURCES

- *Solo: On Her Own Adventure,* edited by Susan Fox Rogers
- *Gutsy Women: Travel Tips and Wisdom for the Road*, Marybeth Bond
- *Women in the Wild: True Stories of Adventure and Connection,* edited by Lucy McCauley
- Outward Bound is a non-profit organization offering outdoor experiential courses all over North America. Find out more at http://www.outwardbound.com

My first commission painting mounted in my friends' home.

Spend Time in Nature

Beautify Your Surroundings

Take some time and beautify an area where you spend a lot of time. This could be your bedroom, apartment, office space, or studio. Create your own sanctuary; surround yourself with things that relax you, please you to look at, energize you, and bring you joy.

- **Beautify your space.** Decorate with art work (paintings or sculptures), your favorite book, pictures of friends and family or pets. Place a stuffed animal, natural stones, shells, or artifacts on a shelf. Use plants and fresh flowers to add beauty and life to your space.
- **Create a calm atmosphere.** Decorate with prayer beads, live bamboo shoots, a running water fountain, or a tibetan singing bowl. Burn incense sticks, aromatherapy, or candles. Set up a fish pond outside or an aquarium inside. Put a small bonsai tree on your desk. Play relaxing background music. (See resources on page 24.)
- **Use the multiple benefits of water.** Water is calming and helps absorb excess radiation from computers and other sources. Put a glass bowl or ceramic jug of water on your desk or coffee table. Place a water fountain near your desk.
- **Establish clean air.** Use an air filter or open the windows for fresh air. keep plants that clean the air such as;climbing tropical plants, spider plants, and aloe vera.

- **Use full spectrum lighting.** Full spectrum lighting aids in stress reduction and promotes good vision. Better yet, open curtains for natural light.
- **Sit comfortably**. Get a comfy work chair with good back support. Put your feet flat on the floor and use a foot stool if necessary. Have your computer eye level and your wrists bent slightly down to the keyboard.
- **Minimize radiation.** Keep hematite beads in your pocket or wear them as an anklet. Hematite is a grounding stone that will fend off computer radiation.
- **Feng Shui your living space.** Feng Shui involves placing furniture and using selected colors for decorating to create harmony, balance, and abundance. (See resources page 24 for books and web sites.)

For several years I worked as an engineering geologist. Although I was fortunate to get outdoors during field work, computer work was necessary to process the data collected. At one particular company I worked for, the office setting included fluorescent lights, dividers to create cubicles, and recycled air. I was adamant to liven up my work space so I decided to bring in a few of my paintings and hang them on the cubicle divider. The two paintings I used to decorate were a set; both were blue and white blended abstract pieces. Everybody enjoyed the added color to the office. I also brought in a huge broad-leafed tropical plant in a ceramic pot, which I placed in the corner of my desk. With the paintings and my plant I created a tropical oasis. My office space was now more personalized and I felt happier writing reports and analyzing data.

♥

"For maximum beauty and tranquility a simple and uncluttered area gives the greatest peace of mind."

- DEB

RESOURCES

- Brighten up your space with vibrant original art, prints, and posters by DEB. Samples for view at www.DEBCreative.com.
- Some relaxation music: *Sounds of Nature* - Ocean Waves, Sounds of the Tropical Rainforest, *ENYA* - Shepherd Moons, The Celts, The Memory of Trees, *Hilary Stagg* - Sweet Return, Beyond the Horizon, *Natural Massage Therapy* - Solitudes, Music for Your Health, *Aeoliah* - Angel Love.
- Full spectrum lighting vendors: www.naturallighting.com and www.fullspectrumsolutions.com.
- *A Master Course in Feng Shui,* Eva Wong
- *Dressing the Whole Person: Nine Ways to Create Harmony & Balance in Your Wardrobe (& Prosperity in Your Life!),* Evana Maggiore
- *Feng Shui: Back to Balance*, Sally Fretwell.
- Feng Shui web sites: www.wofs.com & www.amfengshui.com.

Turn Down Life's Volume

Every day we are subjected to continual noise - both internally and externally. Our minds chatter constantly; "Should I do this? Could I do that? What will they think? This won't work! I can't do it." Similarly, our outside world is chaotically rushing around us at a million miles an hour: cars rushing by, radios and TVs blaring, and cell phones ringing. When we consciously choose to turn down the volume, both inside and outside ourselves, we allow time for our minds, our bodies, and our spirits to rest and re-connect.

♥

- **Take a daily quiet time.** Set a time each day to slow down, unplug from the frenzy, and relax. Sit silently and practice conscious breathing or yoga. Take a ten minute walk in silence. Take a ten minute nap.
- **Slow down.** Ask yourself; "Why am I rushing?" Life is not an emergency.
- **Limit today's 'To Do' list.** Keep the list down to five items or less. Ask yourself; "How can I do less?"
- **Unplug from the media.** Cut down on the amount of times you listen to the news and watch TV. Turn off your car radio. Stop reading trashy girl magazines. Reduce your visits to the mall.
- **Listen to the natural world.** Sounds such as falling rain, ocean waves, a river running, wind blowing through trees, a purring cat, and the chirping of birds are all soothing and therapeutic.

- **Designate a set silent time in your home.** Have every-one in your home agree to be completely quiet for a set time period a chosen day. For this period, everyone in the home would refrain from talking and turn off all stereos, comput-ers, radios, TVs, and noise producing machines.
- **Practice awareness.** During your day make a point of tak-ing moments out to notice <u>where you are</u> and <u>what you are doing</u>. For example, when you are waiting in line at the bank, stand up straight and breathe deeply in and out through your nose. Notice the people around you, feel your feet on the ground, and listen to all the sounds of activity going on.

My friend Chantelle and I get together every year for a camping trip. (See the photograph on page ii.) As part of our experience we mutually agree on a designated silent time each day during our retreat. Last year we chose to remain in silence from 7:00 p.m. each evening until morning. During this time we continued our evening activities; walking in proximity to the campsite, sit-ting together by the fire, reading, journal writing, and preparing dinner. However, we did all of these things in silence. The quiet allowed us time to be together and connect on a different level than we would normally achieve by talking. Each morning we always felt rejuvenated and energized.

♥

"You have nowhere to go and nothing to get. Turn off the noise and what you are looking for is right here. The secret is to quiet the mind."
-source unknown

RESOURCES

- *The Power of Now,* Ekhart Toole
- *Sidhartha,* Herman Hess
- The *Key and the Name of the Key is Willingness,* Cheri Huber
- *Don't Hurry Be Happy: 650 ways to slow down and enjoy life,* Ernie Zelinski

Micro Jack and Angie Baby found (guilty!) playing in the home/office inbox.

Live Like a Cat - Relax!

Cats are wonderful animals - relaxed, agile, flexible, and content. We can learn so much about in-the-moment living from cats.

♥

- **Take a cat nap.** To rejuvenate your energy a ten minute naps is perrrfect!
- **Stretch.** Take breaks from your work and stretch your arms, legs, and back.
- **Play.** Add some fun to your day: watch clouds, explore a garden or lie in tall grass, tulip fields, sunflowers, or a cornfield. See "Play with Kids" on page 61 for more playful ideas.
- **Seek out warmth.** Lie or sit near a window that gets the sun. Saunas, hot baths, hot tubs, sun beds, and hot rock massages are excellent ways to warm up a cold body.
- **Be affectionate.** Cuddle with a friend, lover, or family member. Get some personal attention in the form of a massage, shiatsu, or bodywork therapy.
- **Eat and drink small amounts all day**. Eat small meals frequently during the day when you're hungry. Drink water often, in small amounts.
- **Be insatiably curious.** Observe the world around you. Watch butterflies and insects.
- **Eat grass.** Wheat and barley grass are readily available as fresh juice, in capsules, or powders. These grasses provide health benefits such as ridding the body of toxins, reducing inflammation, aiding in cellular regenerations, and strength-

ening body tissues. They have also been used to treat arthritis, bruises, burns, cancer, and constipation.

- **Be in the moment.** Whatever task you are currently undertaking, do this with *all* of your attention. Just like a cat watching a mouse, in that moment nothing else exists except the mouse.

Micro Jack and Angie Baby are the resident cats where I live. They spend their days sleeping in sunny windowsills, meowing when they want food, and rubbing up against me before jumping up to sit on my lap. Jack is still a baby and likes to chase bottle caps for fun. When I throw a bottle cap across the room, he actually picks it up with his mouth and brings it back! He then drops the bottle cap at my feet and meows to encourage me to throw it again. Angie is older and calmer and doesn't take nonsense from anyone. She meows loudly every morning for her special tin food and won't take no for an answer. Both cats remind me to be at ease and in the moment. They are always present, curiously checking out what's going on, but rarely getting ruffled or upset by anything. Often they snuggle up on a sofa chair together and lick each other's ears. It's heartwarming to watch. Mostly they take naps and hang out. Our house rule here is that if you are feeling stressed out the best solution is to play with or pet the cats. Cats make wonderful 'stress sumps' - you can feel your stress melt away as the cat purrs on your lap.

♥

"Slow down and enjoy life. It's not only the scenery you miss by going too fast - you also miss the sense of where you are going and why."
-Eddie Cantor

RESOURCES

- *Cats,* the musical by Andrew Loyd Webber.
- Adopt a cat - contact your local SPCA.
- Pet and play with your friend's cat.
- *Flying Colors Aromatherapy and Massage*, located on Gabriola Island, British Columbia, Canada, offer an amazing salt scrub, hot smooth basalt rock massage, and aromatherapy massage. This experience takes place in a hand built gazebo with a skylight allowing you to look at the sky and overhanging Arbutus trees. Contact Anita Kalnay at 250-247-9140 or RR1 S14 C9T, Gabriola Island, British Columbia, Canada, V0R 1X0.

"Our deepest fear is not that we are inadequate.

Our deepest fear is that we are powerful
beyond measure.

It is our light, not our darkness that frightens us.

We ask ourselves, who are we to be brilliant,
gorgeous, talented and fabulous?

Actually, who are you not to be?

You playing small doesn't serve the world.

There is nothing enlightened about shrinking
so other people won't feel insecure around you...

And as we let our light shine,
we unconsciously give other people
permission to do the same.

As we are liberated from our own fear,
our presence automatically liberated others!"

- Nelson Mandela

Live Like a Cat - Relax!

Part Two - Consider This

Hot steam rising from the earth in northern Iceland.

On this three month cycling trip,
I let go of schedules
and other people's expectations.
Cycling in Iceland taught me how to enjoy my own company.
I lived my dream and found a deep strength within.

Let Go

Holding on to a person or situation that no longer serves us often results in worry, anger, physical stress, and tension in the body. By letting go of whatever is no longer contributing positively to our lives, we let go of adjoining negative emotions that harm us. By letting go, we liberate ourselves, and can move on.

♥

- **Acknowledge what is no longer contributing to your happiness.** Are you holding onto a particular person or a memory? A situation from the past? A painful memory?
- **Talk about it.** Talk to a friend, a relative, a counselor or therapist. Ask for help, let someone help you.
- **Write about it.** Write out how you feel. This could be in point form, notes, or in poems.
- **Have compassion for yourself.** Grief is a natural side effect of loss and may appear as despair, disbelief, anger, or shock. The process of letting go and moving on will take time, forgiveness, love, perspective, and humor.
- **Shower it away.** Using your favourite soap or body scrub, physically wash away negative feelings and memories.
- **Throw it away.** Make your own ritual of throwing away painful memorabilia into the trash.
- **Burn it.** After you have written out what you need to let go of, take the piece of paper and ceremoniously light it on fire.
- **Change the old memory.** Associate the painful memory with something quirky or humorous that will make you laugh every time you think back to that person or situation.

- **Eliminate *'should have, would have, could have'* in your daily vocabulary.** Replace these words with *'I can, I will*, I *choose, I am willing*, and I *am capable*'. Choose to live today with no regrets.
- **Eat foods to help the process of letting go.** Foods high in fiber such as apples, brown rice, flax seeds, and green vegetables stimulate the digestive system. Whole foods also build the immune system.
- **Take natural remedies.** St. John's Wart is known to relieve nervous exhaustion and insomnia. Juice from borage leaves and blossoms helps to overcome sad feelings.
- **Use aromatherapy.** Lavender aromatherapy warms the heart and steady the emotions.

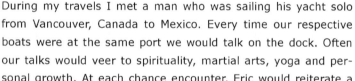

During my travels I met a man who was sailing his yacht solo from Vancouver, Canada to Mexico. Every time our respective boats were at the same port we would talk on the dock. Often our talks would veer to spirituality, martial arts, yoga and personal growth. At each chance encounter, Eric would reiterate a story of two monks on a journey. I never knew if he simply forgot he had already told me the story, or if he was trying to teach me the importance of letting go as I moved forward. The story went like this: Two monks walked a journey together on foot. During their travels they came across a river intersecting their path. As they approached the rushing water, a young woman stood at the river's edge. She asked the older monk, "Would you kindly carry me across the river?" The older monk obliged and carried the young maiden across the river, setting her down on the other side. The two monks then continued their journey. Several miles later the younger monk questioned his elder about his actions, "You have made vows of chastity in becoming a monk, did you not break these in carrying this woman?" The older monk smiled and responded to his young friend, "I put her down at the other side of river, yet you are still carrying her." What we continue to carry on our minds can be a heavy burden on our souls.

**"My barn having burned to the ground
I can now see the moon."**
-J. Stone

RESOURCES
- *A Women's Guide to Living Alone - Ten Ways To Survive Grief and Be Happy,* Pamela Stone
- *Why People Don't Heal and How They Can,* Caroline Myss
- Online support for dealing with grief: www.griefnet.org

A lone sailboat seen as we headed out to sea, the beginning of a three-month sailing voyage from Canada to Mexico.

Rough seas taught me to be 'willing to do whatever it takes' to make my dream come true. Calm days and smooth sailing provided hours to think and reflect.

Let Go

Stop Worrying

Worrying is a negative and destructive habit, both to your mind and body. Worrying keeps your mind overly active, your breath shallow and rigid, and your shoulders bunched up. When you let go of your worries you free up your mind and relax your body. This results in greater energy and awareness.

- **Write each of your worries on little pieces of paper.** Put the papers in a hat or a bowl. When you're ready, pull out *one* piece of paper. Make a plan to deal with that single issue today.
- **Get logical and sort out the problem.** Describe in detail the why, how, when, where, and what of the situation you are worried about. Think of ways to alleviate the problem.
- **Be proactive.** If there is something you can do to help or change the situation. *Do it now*!
- **Live within the day.** Do the best you can within today - it is all you can realistically and practically do. Trust that when you give your best today you ensure a bright tomorrow.
- **Appreciate what you *do* have.** Put your situation in perspective. For the one thing you lack, or that you are worrying about, write out a list of five things you do have.
- **Accept change.** Constant change is the one thing you can count on for the rest of your life. Surrender to it.

- **Release "What's next?" and think "What's NOW?"**
  Instead of focusing miles or days ahead, focus on the current task at hand and do your best.
- **Use homeopathy.** Tablets of *Arsenicum Alb. 6X* homeopathy can be taken five nights consecutively under the tongue before bed time to alleviate teeth grinding caused from stress and worry.
- **Use aromatherapy.** Patchouli aromatherapy helps with clarifying problems and thought processes.

♥

Last year I decided to live in Mexico for three months. I resolved to take this time to write, paint, practice martial arts, plan out my creative company, and enjoy the sun. I had come to Mexico with some savings and hoped that it would be enough to last for this time. The expense for my room, food, taekwondo classes, plus other miscellaneous expenses, however, started to deplete my savings. I started to panic - yes worry - about money. I wanted so much to stay in Mexico and I knew I would have to find either a cheaper way to live or a source of income to allow me to stay. Getting a work permit was impossible so I knew I had to be innovative to make it work. The first thing I did was walk down the docks of the local marinas and talked to many of the American boat owners, asking if anyone would like their boat 'house sat' while they were away. It turned out that a couple was just leaving and would be happy to let me live aboard their boat in exchange that I varnish the deck teak wood. Now that I had a place to live, I decided to search for work to buy food and sundries. I continued to walk the docks and also the dry-dock asking if help was needed - cleaning and repairing boats or baby sitting kids. I got a job in which I earned twenty dollars by scrubbing the galley of an old boat. That was enough money to keep me going for two weeks. I earned some more petty cash by baby sitting. I also brought in some money by writing freelance articles for a local American tourist 0paper. Hence with my free living situation, a modest income, and by eating the most basic foods - beans, rice, and vegetables - I managed to live and stay in Mexico for three months. I used my initial worry to take action and change my situation.

"We are so privileged that we have to ignore vast areas of our lives in order to pick out just those things that aren't the way we want then to be."

- Cheri Huber

RESOURCES

- *Don't Sweat the Small Stuff,* Richard Carlson
- *How to Stop Worrying and Start Living,* Dale Carnegie
- Pop song *Don't Worry, Be Happy*
- This website lightheartedly discusses why we should not worry: http://www.vaxxine.com/steveb/whywory.htm

Don't Give Up

Living your dreams will not always easy. You will undoubtedly meet many challenges and obstacles along the way. As you continue to keep your goals and purpose in your heart, persevering through hard times, the journey will teach you valuable lessons. These lessons in self-discovery will be well worth the journey.

♥

- **Repeat a powerful slogan during hard times.** Put a sticky note on the dash board of your car, your refrigerator, bathroom mirror, or next to your compute, reading;
    [1]*"I am willing to do whatever it takes"*
    "Ready or not, I am doing it anyway"
    "Winners never quit, quitters never win"
    "I act in spite of my fear"
    "Its only as hard as I make it"
    "Failure is not an option"
    "I will succeed in spite of anything"
    "I will never surrender"
    "Carpe diem!" (seize the day!)
- **Break up goals into baby steps.** For example, if you are writing a book, commit to writing the first line of one chapter, then follow through. Do a little bit every day.
- **Congratulate yourself on small accomplishments.** If you set your goal to water the plants in the morning and then follow through and do it, acknowledge your achievement and applaud yourself for following through.

- **Model somebody who is doing what you want to do.** Ask your mentor questions to get a sense of how they achieved their success. Post up a picture of your role model to remind you what you are working towards. Think "If they can do it, I can do it."
- **It's not *what* you do, the power lies in *how* you do it.** Whatever it is you have undertaken, the most important part is the process...the actually 'doing' of it. The outcome of your original goal may change. However, the knowledge, lessons, and courage gained from *the process of not giving up* are a prize gained in personal growth.
- **Take some *time out* when a situation is difficult.** Step back and re-assess. Ask yourself: am I learning a valuable lesson here or is it time to change course? Continue with awareness, respecting your inner guidance.

The biggest dream I ever conceived was to cycle tour alone around Iceland. During grade ten geography classes my teacher showed slide pictures of glaciers and mountains from Iceland. Her vivid descriptions of the natural formations and geology excited my interest and never left my mind. I was so excited and yet simultaneously afraid of the idea, I had to make the decision to dive in and go for it, regardless of my fears. I started by writing in my journals and talking to friends about my idea of cycling in Iceland. Over time, my thoughts and ideas turned into little actions, small baby steps towards making this dream a reality. I started learning how to repair my bike at a local community bike shop. Piece by piece I replaced, as well as fine tuned, all the components of my bike. I wrote to the Icelandic tourist center for information asking about road and weather conditions. I wrote a geology term paper on glacial outburst floods, known in Icelandic as jökulhaup's. The summer before my university graduation, I knew that if I didn't go on this trip now, I might never do it. Without stopping to think further, I bought my ticket and announced I was going!

Two days after my arrival in Iceland a young woman close to my age rode her loaded bicycle into the campground where I was recuperating from the flight and adjusting to this new land. Alexis was at the end of her trip, having spent the past month cycling around Iceland. That evening we made dinner together over my Coleman stove and talked. She answered many of my questions, squelched my fears and encouraged me. Looking back, I feel she was sent to me as an omen to remind me that if she could do it, so could I. Alexis was the only other woman I met who was biking solo in Iceland that summer.

I spent three months bike touring solo around one of the most beautiful and untouched countries I have ever seen. I met amazing and supportive people from all walks of life and from all corners of the world. I cycled hundreds of kilometers, dodged diving birds, and combated howling winds. I sang out loud on my bike past farms, mountains, and glaciers. I learned to love my own company and camping alone little spots I'd pick out in the brush away from the road. Above all, I learned to conquer my fear of traveling alone and living my dream by *just doing it*.

"How you do anything is how you do everything"
-Cheri Huber

RESOURCES
- Anthony (Tony) Robbins - motivational tapes, books, seminars and more, http://www.tonyrobbins.com
- Inspirational movies: *Man of Honor* and *Dead Poet's Society*
- Pop song: *"I get knocked down and I get up again"* Tub thumping by Chumbawumba
- *Mastery-The Keys to Success and Long-Term Fulfillment,* George Leonard

Be Yourself - Be Confident!

Being yourself means living your truth, not bothering to impress other people, and sticking to your values. When you are honest with yourself, not compromising the true you, life flows and true success if yours.

♥

- **Fake it 'till you make it.** Imagine speaking, moving, and breathing with confidence. Visualize the ultimate you. As you put your energy into this goal, you will create it.
- **Stop comparing yourself to others.** You are unique with your own special qualities and talents. Nobody in the world is exactly like you or has the gifts you have.
- **Write out five things you love about yourself.** If you find this difficult, ask a good friend to help you write down positive things about yourself. Check back on this list when you're having a bad day.
- **Love your body unconditionally.** Photocopy the certificate on page 58, fill it in, sign it, and post it where you will see it everyday. This is your pledge to love your body.
- **Keep commitments to yourself.** When you make a goal or resolution, you will feel better about yourself when you follow through and complete it. Start today by committing to do something small and following through.
- **Live your truth.** In each situation you encounter, ask yourself, "*Is this true for me?*" Listen to your inner guidance and respect that answer.

- **Express yourself.** Nobody knows more than you how you are feeling and what you need to make it through the day. Let people in your life support you by telling them what you need.
- **Maintain the three pillars.** Get enough to *eat*, enough *sleep*, and enough *exercise* on a regular basis. When you look after yourself, maintaining your energy and a positive mind set is much easier then if you are neglecting yourself.
- **Use natural therapies.** Myrrh aromatherapy offers a sense of well being, confidence, and helps to ease fear.

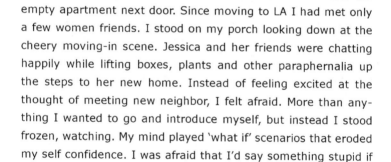

For weeks I'd hoped that another woman would move into the empty apartment next door. Since moving to LA I had met only a few women friends. I stood on my porch looking down at the cheery moving-in scene. Jessica and her friends were chatting happily while lifting boxes, plants and other paraphernalia up the steps to her new home. Instead of feeling excited at the thought of meeting new neighbor, I felt afraid. More than anything I wanted to go and introduce myself, but instead I stood frozen, watching. My mind played 'what if' scenarios that eroded my self confidence. I was afraid that I'd say something stupid if I went to say hello. But even with all the worst case scenarios I could imagine, I was more tired of the prospect of having very few women friends living close by. I went and offered my help to

Be Yourself - Be Confident!

move boxes. The girls were so happy to feel that people in this neighborhood were friendly that they welcomed me immediately. We finished the job faster with all the hands and afterwards sat in Jessica's new kitchen eating cookies and drinking sodas. I was glad I took the risk and introduced myself.

"Finish each day and be done with it. You have done what you could; some blunders and absurdities no doubt crept in; forget them as soon as you can. Tomorrow is a new day; you should begin it well and serenely."
- Ralph Waldo Emerson

RESOURCES
- *The Artists Way,* Julia Cameron
- *Wild Succulent Women,* SARK
- *Getting in Touch With Your Inner Bitch,* Elizabeth Hilts
- Feldenkrais Method helps improve self image by teaching Functional Integration® and Awareness Through Movement®.

Sometimes I am like an electric kettle, plugged into the drama of my life, heating up with my own anger.

When I'm almost boiling, I visualize myself unplugging, and cooling down.

Transform Your Anger

Anger often arises from situations you feel you don't have any control over. This emotion contains a tremendous amount of energy and what's important is how you deal with it. By being aware and conscious of your feelings and dealing with them effectively at the time they arise, you can save yourself future regret and suffering.

♥

- **Acknowledge your feelings.** However you feel is OK. Write it out. Go outside and vent. Cry. Sometimes it feels great to say, "*I feel angry!*", "*I'm jealous*", or "*It's not fair.*"
- **Release your rage in a neutral setting.** Beat up a bag at the gym, go for a run or a bike ride, or punch pillows. Talk to a supportive friend or scream outside in a wide open space.
- **Breathe slowly and count down from ten to one.** Focus on the out breathe and blow out all your anger.
- **Stretch.** Anger makes us tense and tied up in knots. Take a minutes and move your body - stretch out all the negative feelings.
- **Use the energy from your anger.** Anger contains a lot of energy, put it to use constructively. Try an idea from "Move Your Body" on page 5, "Write a Journal" on page 77, "Start a Project" on page 81, or "Get Rid of Something" on page 85.
- **Acknowledge your mind chatter.** Your mind will label events, people, and things telling you, "This is bad." Our minds often make things worse than they are by judging it. Say to your mind, "Thank you for sharing" and then dismiss

the negative mind chatter. By acknowledging your mind and not letting it control you, you can choose a more peaceful reality.

- **Check in regularly with the people in your life.** Have regular talks with your friends, co-workers, kids, and loved ones. Don't let tensions build up by keeping your feelings bottled up.

- **Drop Expectations.** Your pre-conceived expectations may have set up the anger you are now experiencing. Accept that people may not always behave how you would like. Let go of wanting to control other people's behavior.

- **Unplug from your anger.** Visualize yourself as an electric kettle. When you are angry you are plugged into the drama of the situation. Watch for the blue spark as you pull the electric cord from the socket and let go of your anger. Feel yourself start to cool down. See page 50.

- **Think positive.** When you are in an situation which is beginning to make you upset, repeat words to yourself such as: *compassion*, *patience*, *love*, and *understanding*.

- **Listen to calming music.** See music resources in the "Beautify Your Surroudings" chapter on page 24.

- **Use aromatherapy.** Put a couple of drops of aromatherapy oil in your bath or aromatherapy pot. Oil of rose is known to dissipate anger. Cedarwood helps to calm aggression.

For several years I've had warts on my feet. After little success of using nearly every natural remedy available I decided to visit a dermatologist. Dr. McDougall is a friendly young doctor and open to alternative methods of healing. In his office we talked about warts and their relationship to energy and emotions. He was very open to this concept and told me that he strongly encouraged his patients to use visualization to help heal themselves. Once, a young boy and his mother came to his office for a wart treatment. As part of the boys' therapy, Dr. McDougall instructed the boy to visualize his warts flying off and landing onto the person or thing he hated, each night before he went to sleep. Several months later as the doctor was going about his work the phone rang an angry mother at the other end of the line. It was the mother of the young boy he had seen several months before. Apparently the boy's warts were gone. He then asked her, "So what's the problem?" She replied that her son's brother was now covered in warts.

♥

**"You will not be punished for your anger,
you will be punished by your anger."**
- Buddha

RESOURCES

- *Dance of Anger,* Harriet Lerner
- *The Tibetan Book of Living and Dying,* Sogyal Rinpoche
- Websites discussing anger and how best to deal with it:
  http://www.apa.org/pubinfo/anger.html and
  www.angermgmt.com.

Stay

When we are uncomfortable our natural tendency is to avoid or fight the situation we encounter. It is often more difficult to stay present and deal with the situation as it is occurring. But when we do, we can walk away freely, no longer carrying the unresolved baggage and issues with us.

♥

- **Notice how you react in an uncomfortable situation.** When you feel uneasy what is your habit? Do you run away, leave, or avoid difficult situations? In order to avoid dealing with important issues do you smoke, drink, or take drugs? When being present is awkward, do you eat or talk excessively, indulge in constant activity, watch TV, or work continuously to avoid what is actually happening? When you feel anxious do you clam up & ignore friends, family, or work associates?
- **When you are aware of how you avoid, learn your lesson.** Understand that there is a lesson associated with the painful feelings in each uncomfortable situation you encounter. When you avoid or fight the situation, you lose the lesson. When you deal with the situation now, you can move on.
- **Replace the old habit of avoiding.** You are brave enough, strong enough and smart enough to deal with *everything* you encounter in your life. Take it one step at a time and do the best you can. Think before you speak and take deep slow breaths to gain clarity.

- **Practice meditation.** Meditation is the art of *staying* in one place while observing your breath and events happening around you while remaining detached and objective. Practicing remaining calm and centered during meditation makes it easier to remain objective when you experience rough times and uncomfortable situations in life.

When life throws a storm your way - physically or emotionally, you must recall that the *true* you is the untouchable spirit residing within your body. Imagine you are swimming in a tropical ocean in the midsts of a storm. You are being thrown around haphazardly by the waves and wind. So you decide to dive down several miles into the ocean. You can breathe underwater and are perfectly comfortable. As you swim beyond the rough surface waters, past fish and kelp, deeper and deeper, you reach still and peaceful waters. The water is warm and you are no longer being thrown around. The deeper you plunge, the quieter and calmer the waters around you become. Looking up you can see bands of sunlight piercing the upper waters. Even as the storm rages at the surface above, deep down below where you remain, it is still and calm. Just like the tranquility at the bottom of the ocean, the spirit residing in your physical body is untouchable by the storm of events around you. You can stay and endure any stressful or difficult situation, while remaining calm within yourself, because your spirit resides in an untouchable place within you.

"[2]It is simple... we are where we should be doing what we should be doing. Otherwise...we would be somewhere else doing something else."
-Richard Stine

RESOURCES

- *Breathing, The Master Key to Self-Healing* and *8 Meditations for Optimum Health,* Andrew Weil, M.D.
- *When Things Fall Apart: Heart Advice for Difficult Times*, *Start Where You Are: A Guide to Compassionate Living,* and *The Wisdom of No Escape*, Pema Chodron. Pema is a Buddhist monk who has written several books and has made several recorded video presentations both teaching Buddhist practice and how it applies to every day life.
- *The Key and the Name of the Key is Willingness*, Cheri Huber

I, _____ agree from this
date forward to love and cherish
myself and my body, just the way I am,
unconditionally. Today I give thanks and know that
I am perfect just the way I am.

Signed_____ Dated_____

Part Three - Try This

My little Mexican Cutie Pie

One of the little girls I played with
while I lived in Mexico.

Play with Kids

Play with Kids

Playing with kids is a stress-free, inspiring, and battery recharging way to spend some time. Kids remind us of how we used to be - fearless, alive, curious, and bundles of endless energy. Hanging out with kids shows us how to live in the moment, relax, and have fun.

♥

- **Play games with kids.** Let the kids tell you what to do! Play games like frozen statues, eye spy, or tag. Participate in kids' street hockey, basketball, soccer, hopscotch, or square ball.
- **Be crazy with kids.** Swing, spin in circles until you're dizzy, or do cartwheels and somersaults. Blow bubbles out the car window or decorate the sidewalk with colored chalk drawings.
- **Get outside with kids.** Build a tree house, make sand castles at the beach, jump rope, pick leaves and flowers to press. Go on a teddy bear picnic.
- **Go on an outing with kids.** Go for a bike ride to a new place. Visit waterslides, a science center, a fair, a zoo, or an aquarium. play paint ball.
- **Help kids.** Volunteer at the children's ward of a hospital, be a big sister, or a foster parent. Teach kids swimming, painting, gymnastics, martial arts, journal writing, making models, or skateboarding. What can you teach kids?

♥

While I was living on a sailboat and crewing down the coast of Mexico, my captain and I stopped at various small town ports to rest and pick up supplies. We always anticipated going ashore as it gave us a chance to stretch our legs and get out of small confined area of the 26′ Columbia sailing vessel. On one of these stops I decided to practice my karate on the beach. As I practiced each sequence of pre-arranged movements, called katas, children from the small remote village nestled in the bay shyly appeared out of nowhere and began watching me. As I continued on with my practice some of the children became braver and crept up to a small stone wall located close to me. Before I knew it, eight or more kids were watching me intently and some of them had started to mimic my moves. By this time, there was no ignoring the little spectators. I decided to switch from practicing my karate to doing some gymnastics - handstands and cartwheels. The kids got the idea and joined in. An hour later the group of us were running, jumping, doing back bends, and somersaults on the beach. By using hand signals and drawing images in the sand, we told each other our about ourselves. I drew a picture of North America and a picture of a sailboat, explaining that I had sailed to Mexico from Canada. The kids drew their names in the sand, pictures of their pets, and then gestured excitedly for me to teach them more gymnastics. We were all full of smiles and laughter by the time I had to board the little inflatable row boat that took me back to my home sailing vessel anchored in their bay. After spending time with these kids, I came back aboard rejuvenated and excited about life. As I sat up through my night watch, steering the boat south, I thought about their bright gleaming brown eyes and eager faces

"[5]There are lives I can imagine without children but none of them have the same laughter and noise."
- Brian Andreas

RESOURCES

- Hang out with your kids, your friends' kids, your neighbor's kids.
- Get to know the child within you.
- A wonderful Internet resource of hundreds of kids games http://www.gameskidsplay.net/
- Become a Big Sister. See websites for more information: http://www.bbbsa.org/ (USA) and http://www.bbsc.ca/ (Canada).

DEB painting in the backyard.

Create a Positive Focus in Your Life

It is so easy to focus on what's wrong and what's not working in our lives. If this negativity is your continual focus, the results in your life will reflect this. Every day you have the choice to see the good that is presenting itself. When you focus on the positive, your life will reflect your beliefs. Dreams and ideas that you may have previously believed not possible, can now be created.

♥

- **Give thanks for each day.** Pray, write out, or vocalize five things that you are grateful for today. You may appreciate the air you breathe, a friend, or your home.
- **Start a project.** Choose to do something that gives you a good feeling every time you do it. I feel great every time I work on a painting. See "Start a Project" on page 81 for project ideas.
- **Repeat positive words or phrases to yourself.** Vocalize positive thoughts and feelings. Post up a phrase:
    - 3"More and more I yield to make peace"
    - "I drop effort and all that I need comes to me"
    - "I lighten up on myself and others"
    - "I choose reconciliation and forgiveness: I let go of the need for revenge"
    - "I acknowledge as my own potential what I strongly admire in others"
    - "Everyone and everything is my teacher"

- **Notice your negative mind chatter.** Pay attention to the continual chatter of your mind's voice. Often we have tape recorders in our head saying things like; "This is not right, I can't do it, he's wrong, she's annoying, this sucks..." Instead of agreeing with the negativity, acknowledge your mind by telling it "thank you for sharing" and let go of the thought.
- **Take each situation as it comes.** Every situation has a challenge - make a point of finding something good about it.
- **Meditate in the morning.** Focus on your breathing, sit still, and listen to the silence around you. By relaxing at the start of the day you create a calm and grounded mind set to carry you through the day.
- **Eat simple, clean, and whole foods.** Food has a tremendous effect on your life outlook and moods. Choose whole foods over refined foods. See "You are What You Eat" on page 13.
- **Listen to upbeat music.** Some of my favorite albums are listed in the resources section at the end of this chapter.

Painting is something I've done for fun and relaxation for many years now. Like many artists, I've always dreamed about selling my paintings and earning an income from my hobby. Shortly after I moved to Los Angeles, my friend Steve came across a little postcard sized painting I had done. The painting consisted of a bright red and orange heart surrounded by blues and whites. I had accidentally left it behind in a mutual friend's truck when moving, and had totally forgotten about it. Steve was now borrowing the same truck and when the art caught his eye he knew it was mine. He called me immediately on his cell phone and asked if I would paint a large four-foot by four-foot painting similar to this small one for his home. (See page 20 for the final heart painting.) I was overjoyed! After that first painting, word of mouth spread and I received several other commissions.

♥

"The grand essentials of happiness are: something to do, something to love, and something to hope for."
- Allan K. Chalmers

RESOURCES
- *Heal Your Body: The Mental Causes for Physical Illness and the Metaphysical Way to Overcome,* Louise L. Hay
- Movie: *Pollyanna*
- http://www.funnytimes.com/
- Upbeat music: Fine Young Cannibals *The Raw and The Cooked*, Madonna *Immaculate Conception*, ABBA *Greatest Hits*, The Best of Van Morrison, The Power of One *Sound Track,* Cat Stevens *Greatest Hits,* and Tom Petty *Greatest Hits.*

My amazing friend Sally

*Sally encouraged me to write down all the
ideas that became
The Little Inspiration Book*

Create a Positive Focus in Your Life

Create a Support Network

Some days you may feel alone or depressed and need something or someone to build your spirits. A support network is
something you create now, so that on those low days when life
seems to have turned against you, you can reach out.

♥

- **Write a list of supportive people in your life.** Think of
  someone you can visit that lives close, someone you can
  write or E-mail, and someone you can phone. Keep this list
  by the phone or computer.
- **Write down three things that support you unconditionally.** Your list could include; going to a sacred place
  where you feel nurtured, reading a good book, or watching
  your favorite movie. You could cuddle with your favorite
  stuffed animal or pet or talk with an encouraging friend or
  family member.
- **Have a girls' night in.** Get together and paint your finger
  and toe nails, make home-made pizza, watch a chick-flick,
  make your own t-shirts, paint underwear designs (my friend
  painted "Go Slow" on her underwear), or make crafts.
- **Create sacred memories.** Keep a scrapbook with photos of
  good times with friends and family, trip photos, or a memo-
  rable event for you. Flip through your collage to get the
  warm fuzzy feeling back.
- **Give what you want to receive.** If you want flowers, give
  them. If you desire friendship, become a friend to someone.

If you want compassion and understanding, show this to other people in your life.

- **Perform random acts of kindness.** Help a new neighbor move in, leave flowers on a stranger's doorstep, write a kind message or quote on the street using sidewalk chalk.
- **Join a club or take a class.** Take a class in yoga, aerobics, sewing, dancing, or swimming. Join a group such as a book club, a women's support group, or bible study.
- **Ask for support when you need it.** Don't be afraid to ask when you need help and support. Life is too short to let others guess how you feel and what you need.
- **Give and receive hugs.** There is nothing like human touch and affection to help heal a wounded soul.

Go into your body and focus on one cell. Within that cell, picture the atoms making it up. Focus on one atom. See the particles of energy that make up the atom. Feel the vibration and energy in these extremely tiny parcels of energy. Realize that this energy not only makes up all your atoms, cells, and your entire body, but also all my atoms, and cells of my body. The ocean, the rocks and the sun are all made from these same atoms. This energy is everything we see around us. We are all of the same essence: energy. Hence we are all connected to all other beings on this planet and the universe. We are not alone, but part of the whole universal energy.

♥

"We are all connected to everyone and everything in the universe. Therefore, everything one does as an individual affects the whole. All thoughts, words, images, prayers, blessings, and deeds are listened to by all that is."

- Serge Kahili King

RESOURCES

- *Chicken Soup for the Soul,* Jack Canfield and Mark Victor Hanson
- An uplifting and motivating novel *The Power of One,* Bryce Courtney
- A supportive website for when you're going through tough emotional times: www.lifechallenges.org
- SARK's Inspirational phone line 1-415-546-3742
- A great chick-flick: *Charlie's Angels* starring Drew Barrymore, Lucy Liu, and Cameron Diaz.

Magazine cuttings I pasted into one of my journals
to remind me of things I want in my life.

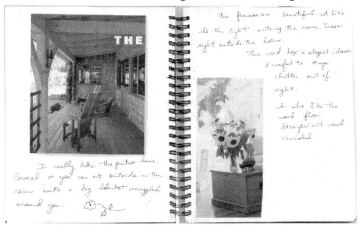

Design Your Life

When you take time out to evaluate what you *really* want in your life, you begin to change your future. Writing out and visualizing your dreams sets the stage for new ideas to become material.

♥

- **Start a goal book.** All you will need is a notebook. Each New Year's Eve, take a clean page in your notebook and head each page with a goal category that works for you. Potential goals could be in the following categories:
    - Finances, work, career, business, or investments.
    - Family & friends, relationships, or home.
    - Spiritual, creative, artistic, writing, or music.
    - Education, learning, or school.
    - Travel, adventure, dreams, or outdoors.

  Beneath your selected category write *specifically* what you intend to accomplish this year.
- **Plan long term.** Draw six columns and label each as follows: six months, one year, two years, five years, ten years and twenty years. Below each column, write out all the things you intend to learn, experience, and achieve within this time. Re-evaluate these goals periodically.
- **Draw a circle.** Write single words within the circle, each word representing what you want in your life right now. Doing this regularly enables you to become aware of what you value and what is most important in your life.

- **Create a Mandala.** A mandala is an ancient circular symbol representing events in your life that have brought you to today and will lead you to your future. To create this powerful art piece choose images that represent your life; past, present, and future. Use your own sketches or drawings, personal photos, cutouts from magazines, individual words or a personal symbol. Assemble the images in a creative fashion, playing with colors and textures. Your final product is an artistic representation of your life.
- **What is your personal definition of success?** Write a statement describing what success is for you.
- **Describe yourself at age seventy.** Write, paint, or draw this 'future you'. Envision where you will live, who will be there with you, what you will you be doing, and how you will look.
- **What if you had only one year to live?** What would you change about your life if you had a limited time to live? What dream would you fulfill? Write about this.
- **Write out your life's mission statement and purpose.** Include what you hope to accomplish within your lifetime, what gifts you hope to leave behind to the world, and the difference your life will make.

The first time I remember meeting Leslie was at a family dinner party at her home. The occasion was to welcome me as I was an old family friend new to the city. I had recently moved to begin my university studies. The last time Leslie and I had met, I had been an infant and Leslie a teenager. Now that we were both adults, Leslie and I connected immediately, and began a relationship that changed my life. During the next six years Leslie and I would often meet late at night after our respective work and school days. She would ask me questions that challenged who I was and what I was doing with my life. One night she asked me, "Deb, what is your life purpose and what do you think you are here on earth to do?" I stared at her blankly. Purpose? I had a purpose? I had never considered it. Leslie showed me how to mold my reality and envision my dreams. She encouraged me to write out my goals each year, as she did with her kids. (See 'Start a goal book' back on page 73.) She introduced me to new books, videos, and ideas that expanded my world. She led me to opportunities that opened my mind and my belief system. Years later I flipped through the first goal book I had written, encouraged and instigated by Leslie. It was a notebook she had given me, in which I had written the details of each of my goals for that year. Looking through the lists, I realized that I had accomplished nearly everything I had set out to do. Among all the gifts I received from Leslie, the most powerful was in learning to make my dreams become reality by writing them out.

♥

"⁴Commit to living your dreams - one day at a time. This is the process that is required to heal our families, our communities and our planet."
-Christiane Northrup, MD

RESOURCES

- *The Seven Habits of Highly Effective People,* Steven R. Covey
- *The Road Less Travelled,* M. Scott Peck
- *One Year to Live,* Stephen Levine
- *The Purpose of Your Life,* Carol Adrienne
- A website showing several examples of mandalas: http://www.jassmine.com/mandala.html

Write a Journal

A journal is a sacred place for you to vent your emotions, sort out frustrations, think things over, plan, dream and create new possibilities and realities. Nearly all the ideas for *The Little Inspiration Book* started as little notes in my journals. You can use your journal as a springboard for making your dreams come true.

There are no rules in journal writing.
Write when it feels right; if that's once a year, in the middle of the night, so be it. Don't worry about spelling or grammar. Here are some suggestions to get you started...

- **Use a notebook without lines.** Lines are limiting and rigid.
- **Use multi colored pens.** Express yourself with different colored pencil crayons, felt pens, or colored ball point pens for your different feelings, thoughts, and ideas. Adding color creates life and energy in your journal.
- **Add neat stuff to your journal.** Paste in postcards and letters, magazine pictures, photos, dried flowers, bus tickets, memos, receipts, or personal sketches. See page 72.
- **Make a wish.** Make a list of some things you would like to do or things you would like to own. I always decorate my wish lists with stars and hearts for good luck.
- **Set five goals for the day.** Do the hardest thing first. Don't add to the list after you've checked something off.

- **Celebrate each accomplishment!** Too often we look at our next 'to do' list without acknowledging what we have already done. Take a moment and put a capital *YES!* next to the completed items from your 'to do' list.
- **Congratulate yourself.** Even some of the littlest things you do have a positive effect on people you come in contact with. This could be a kind word you said to a friend or colleague, washing laundry for your family, a letter you wrote to someone, a meal you cooked for others, a friend you listened to, or the time you took to share your dreams and stories with others. Write about something you've done to make a positive difference in the world today.
- **Write a list of what you are thankful for.** There is so much to notice and be thankful for every day. I often write that I am thankful for the sun, water to drink, and fresh air.
- **Write down how you feel right now.** Your journal is a place to vent out your frustrations. Feeling crappy? Write about it!
- **Write down your childhood dream.** When you were little, what did you want to be when you grew up? Recall the details.
- **Recall last night's dream.** You can gain an incredible amount of inner wisdom and life direction via your dreams. Dreams can contain messages or answers to questions. Start taking advantage of this great resource - your inner guidance - by writing about your dreams when you wake up in the morning.

Several years ago I started writing in my journal about the idea of working as crew aboard a large sailing vessel. I had seen the movie 'White Squall' and loved the images of the crew climbing up the mast, eating hot dinners in the galley, and standing watch on deck as waves pounded over the side of the boat. The idea began to grow from within my journals. While flipping through magazines, I cut out pictures of large boats I thought I would like to work on. Seeing those boat pictures would remind me of my dream. I wrote about the type of people I would love to sail with. I drew maps in my journal of places I would like to visit. I talked to sailors from the local sailing club who gave me advice on books to read and courses to take - all of which I wrote down in my journal. I got on the Internet and searched for 'crew wanted' advertisements and made lists of the best web sites to check on a regular basis. My efforts paid off and I found a boat sailing from Vancouver to San Francisco. After meeting the captain and agreeing to crew, I began the first leg of a 1,200 miles journey sailing down the west coast of North America from Canada to Mexico. I worked as crew for room and board and moving from boat to boat made my way down the coast to Mexico. I cooked meals half upside-down, stayed on watch through a storm, swam naked in deep blue waters a hundred miles off the coast, survived seasickness, heard incredible stories and met amazing people. The key element in making my sailing adventure real was the writing about it and planning it in my journal.

♥

"Over and over again, as soon as I've become clear on what it is I want, the circumstances I need to get it are miraculously available to me"
-Elaine St. James

RESOURCES

- *Spilling Open* and *Brave on the Rocks,* Sabrina Ward Harrison
- *Writing Down the Bones* and *Wild Mind; Living the Writers Life,* Nathalie Goldberg

Start a Project

Having a personal project that you can do on your own is like having a friend you can always count on. There are times when plans fall through and you are left on your own. This time is an opportunity to work on a project.

- **Make a list of some projects you would like to do.** Be sure to include things you can do with yourself. You could:
    - Paint, draw, sketch or sculpt.
    - Write a short story, a letter, or a poem.
    - Plan a trip or adventure.
    - Make an album of your photos.
    - Start a needlepoint, sewing, or quilting project.
    - Learn an instrument.
    - Read a book or explore the Internet.
    - Plant a garden or herb pots on a window sill.
    - Build a model airplane, boat, or car.
- **Create a Gold Book.** This is a personalized notebook for your golden ideas in. Take a plain notebook and paint it gold (gold spray paint works well). Fill in each page over time as ideas come up. Include sections for activities to do alone or with friends such as:
    - Places to visit, books to read, movies to watch, things to make, money making ideas and projects, or adventurous dreams.

Often I'll keep a page consisting of a list of things I want to do with a particular friend. Every time we get together, we check our page in my gold book then choose an idea. Once you have accomplished your idea or project, put a gold star next to it and celebrate its completion!

- **Assemble a reference book.** Your personal reference book is a binder containing all the significant documents in your life - achievements, articles, job reference letters, school awards, diplomas, certificates, and publications. This book is all about you and your accomplishments. You'll need:
  - a three-ring binder   - plastic covers (8$1/2$″ x 11″)
  - all your certificates.

  Put the certificates in the plastic covers and then into your binder. Look through and give yourself a pat on the back for all the work you put in to achieve these things. Refer back to this binder whenever you don't feel 'good enough'.

- **Start an inspirational quote book.** Whenever you read something that inspires you, jot it down in a special note-book, your inspirational quote book. When it's raining down on your life and you've forgotten the joy in living, pick up your book and read through the quotes you've jotted down. Every chapter in this book has a quote, choose your favorites and write these in your quote book.

Once upon a time my parents bought a new refrigerator. As I watched the appliance men bringing in our new purchase ideas sprang to my mind about the refrigerator box. Reluctantly, after asking and then begging, my mom let me keep the refrigerator large cardboard box. I excitedly set it up in our living room and then began the project of creating my indoor club house. I started by cutting out doors and windows. I used the excess cardboard pieces to create shelves inside. I then used crayons to decorate my new house. Inside I dragged in pillows, blankets and many of my stuffed animals. Once I was fully set up, to his chagrin, I brought in the family cat. I spent hours in my cardboard fort having such a wonderful time I remember this project to this day!

♥

**"Whatever you can do or dream, begin it.
Boldness has genius, power and magic in it."**
-Göethe

RESOURCES

- *Wish Craft,* Barbara Sher
- *Manifest Your Destiny,* Wayne Dyer
- A wonderful Internet resource for quotes:
  http://www.quoteland.com

A desolate yet beautiful scene along the West Coast Trail Vancouver Island, British Columbia, Canada.

I first hiked this trail with my father and some friends at the age of sixteen. I returned ten years later for a totally different experience and hiked the 74 km (50 mile) trail alone.

Get Rid of Something

Out with the old, in with the new. Moving the old energy out of your life by getting rid of old stuff, allows room for a new healthy flow of energy into your life. Getting rid of excessive clutter can free up space, time, and money as well as feel liberating. By owning less, you will have less to maintain, protect, worry about, and care for. Less is definitely more!

♥

- **Throw out the clutter from your house.** Clutter includes broken trinkets and nick knacks, old newspapers and magazines, junk mail, excess plastic bags, un-used exercise equipment, old make-up, broken elastic bands, unused toys, broken TV, radio and appliances, broken or unused kitchen tools, broken pencils, empty pens, and anything that you have not used for more than a year.
- **Ditch duplicates.** Duplicates are things you have more than one of such as cars, bikes, toothbrushes, empty flowerpots, hairbrushes, belts, hats, hair accessories and books.
- **Give away old stuff.** Donate old books and magazines to your public library. Give old clothes, your old computer, your old VCR or video game machine, unused blankets, linen, and towels to charity.
- **Mail it away.** Send items you no longer want or need as a surprise gift to a friend. This could include books, old jewelry, tupperware, toys, or clothing.

- **Clean out your fridge and kitchen cupboards**. Throw out all the junk food, rancid oils, old rotting food. Scrub out all the dust and dirt. Clean up and start fresh.
- **Recycle.** Recycle glass bottles, cans, paper, plastic bags, tetra packs and cardboard.
- **Get rid of unnecessary negativity in life.** Purge people and things that do not contribute positively to your life.

My friend James has a very Zen policy: whenever he gets something new, he gets rid of something old. This way he stops acquiring more and more stuff. I love this idea and apply it regularly in my life. In particular, when I'm having a bad day, I go through everything I own and get rid of things I haven't used for a while or don't really need. I always feel better after I drop off a huge bag at the local charity. Getting rid of junk is a wonderfully therapeutic process.

"To acquire not things, but experiences"
- a mountaineering magazine

RESOURCES

- *Simplify your life* and *Inner Simplicity*, Elaine St. James
- *The Simple Living Guide,* Janet Luhrs
- Online support for simplifying your life:www.simpleliving.net

Become Financially Empowered

Many of us don't know how much money we have in our checking accounts; we aren't saving regularly, and we know very little about investing. When is comes to money, knowledge is power. Knowing more about money creates more choices and greater freedom in our lives.

♥

Become pro-active in your relationship with money.
Implement one or all of the following ideas each month...

- **Think positively about money.** Instead of thinking, "I can't afford it." Change your thought process to, "How can I afford it?" This way you are an active participant in creating your dreams.
- **Trust the flow of money.** Money comes and goes just like the flow of a river, hence the name 'currency'. Sometimes the river floods, sometimes it runs dry. Trust that you will always have money when you need it.
- **Write out your financial goals.** What are you saving up for in the short and long term?
- **Define what financial success is to you.** My personal definition of financial success is to have put away enough money so as to live entirely off the interest of my savings. What defines your financial success?
- **Put away 10% of everything you earn - and don't touch it!** Money set aside gives you choices and freedom you would not have otherwise had.

- **Purchase Assets not liabilities.** Assets are investments you own that make you money. Liabilities are things you buy that cost you money. Instead of purchasing liabilities such as another lotto ticket, a new car, new clothes, or furniture, buy things that will earn you money in the future. Assets include savings bonds, stocks, mutual funds, investment property, equity in your home, your own business, your own product, or an idea you have patented.
- **Keep track of how much you spend.** Learn how much money you need to live happily each month. Where is all your money going? Where could you cut down and save more?
- **Balance your checkbook regularly.** Know how much money you have in the bank at any given time.
- **Freeze your credit card.** Take your credit cards, put them in a plastic container, fill it with water, and leave it in your freezer. The next time you decide to make a credit card purchase you will have to thaw the ice. Use the time to think, "Do I really need to buy this?"
- **Learn more about finances.** Read books, magazines, and newspapers. Look for topics about investing, stocks, and-bonds. Watch and listen to special TV and radio shows about managing your money. Talk to people that know more than you do.
- **Cross your T's.** Ancient folklore says that thoroughly crossing your t's while handwriting promotes financial abundance.

"Today I am going to give you eighty thousand dollars". My dad sat down on the sofa across from me. I had been asking him questions and was worried about money and meeting my future financial goals. "This money will be directly deposited into your bank account. There are a few rules that go along with the money, they are as follows. You can do anything you want with it, except for two things. You cannot save it nor can you invest it. At the end of the day, the remaining money that you do not spend will be taken from your account." My dad smiled and I leaned forward listening intently. He continued, "The following day another $80,000 will again be deposited in your bank account. The same rules will apply - no saving, no investing. At the end of the day the unspent money will be gone. This will continue for the rest of your life." My mind raced. What would I do with all this money? Would I change anything I am doing now? I would no longer have to worry, that was for sure! My dad explained; "Deb, this $80,000 represents your life. Every day you get a chance to live your life to the fullest and enjoy it. You never know when your life will end. Money is simply a tool to be used wisely and enjoyed. You can use or not. But when it comes down to it, the unused $80,000 in the bank will do you no good at all when you leave this earth. You cannot take it with you." My dad's story reminds me to keep money and my life in perspective.

"The real measure of your wealth is how much you'd be worth if you lost all your money."
-Anonymous

RESOURCES

- Look for listings in your local paper for continuing education courses about finances and money management. Also check for classes at the local community center, school, or college.
- Check out the financial section of your local public library for books, audiocassettes, and videotapes on money managment.
- *Rich Dad Poor Dad,* Robert Kiyosaki and www.richdad.com
- *The Wealthy Barber*, George S. Clason
- *The Richest Man in Babylon*, David Chilton
- *Your Money or Your Life,* Vicky Robin and Jo Dominguez
- *You Have More Than You Think,* David and Tom Gardner (The Motley Fools) and www.motleyfool.com

Permissions

1 - Phrases quoted in "Don't Give Up" on page 43; "*I am willing to do whatever it takes*", "*Ready or not, I am doing it anyway*", "*Failure is not an option*", "*I will succeed in spite of anything*" with permission from T. Harv Eker, The Enlightened Warrior Training Camp, © 2000. For further information on The Enlightened Warrior Training Camp and other Peak Potentials courses and camps, E-mail details@peakpotentials.com, visit their website at www.peakpotentials.com or call (604) 983-3344.

2 - Sentence quoted in "Stay" on page 55; "It is simple... we are where we should be doing what we should be doing. Otherwise...we would be somewhere else doing something else." with permission from Richard Stine.

3 - Phrases quoted in "Create a Positive Focus in Your Life" on page 65; "More and more I yield to make peace", "I drop effort and all that I need comes to me", "I lighten up on myself and others", "I choose reconciliation and forgiveness: I let go of the need for revenge", "I acknowledge as my own potential what I strongly admire in others", and "Every one and every thing is my teacher" with permission from *How to Be An Adult* by David Richo and Paulist Press, www.paulistpress.com, © May 1991.

4 - Sentence quoted in "Design Your Life" on page 73; "Commit to living your dreams - one day at a time. This is the process that is required to heal our families, our communities and our planet." with permission of Christiane Northrup, MD, *Women's Bodies, Women's Wisdom*, Bantam © 1998.

5 - Sentence quoted in "Play with Kids" on page 61; "There are lives I can imagine without children but none of them have the same laughter and noise" with permission of Brian Andreas and Story People.

Deb currently lives in Hermosa Beach, California where she spends her time writing and painting. She is currently writing the story of her summer cycle touring solo in Iceland. Her paintings and other creative products are available at www.debcreative.com.

The Little Inspiration Book - Order Information

Telephone 1-250-383-6864 or 1-888-232-4444.

Mail orders Trafford Publishing, Suite 6E, 2333 Government Street, Victoria, B.C. V8T 4P4, CANADA.

Fax 1-250-383-6804

Order On-line http//www.trafford.com

Email bookstore@trafford.com

Please note:
- Shipping and Handling applies to all books shipped.
- Payments accepted: Visa, Master Card, American Express, cheque, or money order. Make cheque payable to *Trafford Publishing*.
- A 40% Discount is available to re-sellers and bulk orders, please inquire before ordering.
- All of Trafford's titles are printed on-demand and are therefore non-returnable.

A great gift idea. Order a copy for a friend *today!*

Printed in the United States
by Baker & Taylor Publisher Services